MISS WINTER'S DEMISE
AND OTHER CRIMES AGAINST POETRY

D1643139

MISS WINTER'S DEMISE
AND OTHER CRIMES AGAINST POETRY

PAUL MINTON

*Rhymes for the whole family and
any pets willing to listen**

*Excludes all cold water and tropical fish

Matador
9 Priory Business Park,
Wistow Road, Kibworth Beauchamp,
Leicestershire. LE8 0RX
Tel: 0116 279 2299
Email: books@troubador.co.uk
Web: www.troubador.co.uk/matador
Twitter: @matadorbooks

ISBN 978 1788038 829

British Library Cataloguing in Publication Data.
A catalogue record for this book is available from the British Library.

Printed and bound in Great Britain by 4edge Limited
Typeset in 11pt Minion Pro by Troubador Publishing Ltd, Leicester, UK

Matador is an imprint of Troubador Publishing Ltd

For Heather and Laura
With all my love

Acknowledgements

As many of these poems were written while in bed, I would like to thank my mattress and pillows for their invaluable support. On the human front, my wife and daughter have given me lots of suggestions, encouragement and cries of despair and I am really grateful for the first two and can only apologise for the latter. A big thank you to my parents for bringing me up properly and my late grandparents for trying to undo their good work (only joking!) A special mention must also go to Helen for reading through my efforts and giving me her sage advice. I think you're all great and I love you to bits. Even the mattress.

Paul Minton
May 2017

Contents

Young Tom

When young Tom had just turned eight,
A duck bit him by a farmyard gate:
Coot or mallard, he couldn't tell,
He only knew it hurt like hell!
But not long after this fowl affair,
Tom grew plumage instead of hair.
His parents thought it still more queer
When they saw two wings appear.
They rushed him to the local docs,
Who said it was just chickenpox
And to cure his feathered skin,
He need only take some aspirin.

Sadly though, it did not suppress
Tom's unexpected birdiness.
The doc advised, with much regret,
The family keep him as a pet
Or else seek out a bird physician,
Who might prevent a full transition.
And so they all went off to see
A recommended veterinary.
"Aha!" he cried, "I have a clue
Your son, in fact, has caught bird flu.
I have right here the antidote
Which, when poured down the throat
(And providing that you keep him warm),
Will return him to his human form."
And so young Tom became once more,
The little boy he was before...
Except that after being attacked,
Tom never spoke: he merely *quacked*.

Where's The Chair?

Whatever's happened to my chair?
I'm sure it used to be right there.
A chair has legs but even so,
It couldn't just get up and go.
Perhaps I'll take a look around
Or read the local 'Lost and Found'.
I suppose a thief might be to blame
And if he is, I want his name!
I loved that chair and though it's gone,
I'll never get another one.
Instead, I'll stand up on my feet
In honour of the stolen seat.
But wait a second, I've been a twit
(Something that happens quite a bit) –
I am mistaken, there is no crime:
I was sitting on it all the time!

The Land of Nod

The Land of Nod is quite bizarre –
It's where the Sleepybobos are:
A forest folk with painted knees,
Who pick off yawns that grow on trees
To make a rather tasty jam,
Which sells for forty winks a gram.
The Rivers Snooze and Slumber pour
Into the placid Sea of Snore,
Where Shuteyes with their stripes and flippers
Swim alongside giant Kippers,
Deep down in waters underneath,
Hunted by fierce Catnap teeth.
The Mattress Mountains rise up proud
And reach right into pillow cloud,
Whilst grazing on their slopes asteep
Are the famous counting sheep,
Each taking turns to jump a fence,
Which must defy all common sense.
This dreamy realm is such a sight,
I go there almost every night;
For when I close my tired eyes,
I'm gently pulled by small Nighnighs
Into this world, both strange and odd,
This sleepy place, this Land of Nod.

AUNTIE
MABEL

Auntie Mabel rides a motorbike;
One day I asked her, "What's it like?"
She said, "It's fast while I go
But when I stop, it's very slow."

The Afterlife Mail

It would be absurd
If you'd ever heard
About *The Afterlife Mail*.
It can only be read
By those who are dead:
The living won't find it for sale.
Inside it features
All manner of creatures
And stories from Heaven and Hell
Like the headless rider,
Who drank too much cider
And ended up legless as well.
There's news about trips
On eerie death ships
Plus Pearly Gate weather reports.
With expert reviews

Of zombie shampoos,
It appeals to spooks of all sorts.
For the newly at rest,
The sports page is best
With results from every event:
Hearse racing at Chester,
Coffin dodging in Leicester,
And phantomweight boxing from Kent.
To get an edition,
There's still the condition
That you've joined the skeleton crew.
In ghostly tedium?
Then contact a medium,
Who will spirit a copy to you.

Why on earth are snails so slow?
Perhaps they've nowhere else to go
And thus they travel round and round,
Leaving patterns on the ground:
Silver trails for us to track,
Going forwards, going back.
But maybe when viewed from the air,
Their slime spells out, 'HELLO UP THERE!'

CROOKED SID

Long ago in the West,
When newspapers obsessed
Over outlaws like Billy The Kid,
There resided a thief
With lopsided teeth,
Who went by the name, Crooked Sid.

Now Sid would just steal
Whatever he'd feel:
A quick *whoosh* and things would be gone.
He once took sheriff's loo
Without leaving a clue
So the Law had nothing to go on.

Never a week went by
When Sid did not try
To rob someone if chance arose.
But he faced a backlash
When the mayor's fine moustache
Was stolen from under his nose.

The townsfolk elected
That cash be collected
And used as a price on Sid's head:
A generous bounty
To all in the county
For catching him living or dead.

Gluing mayor's 'tache to his lip,
Sid gave them the slip:
A disguise that worked real great.
Escaping to Memphis,
He married a dentist
And soon, he and his teeth had gone straight.

Winging it

"My word!" I said when first I spied
A sheep with wings which flew outside.
But that's not all for then I saw
A flock of ten or maybe more.
A border collie was in pursuit:
Upon his back, a parachute
And while he chased them through the air,
A pony glided past, I swear.
He looped the loop with total ease
As coloured smoke blew from his knees.
Whatever next, I could not say
But then a cow swooped my way.
To its udders, a farmer's wife
Was clinging helplessly for life.
And last of all, some goats flapped by
So who knows, perhaps pigs MIGHT fly!

Canterbury's Tail

In a house down a road called Gideon's Way
Lived an assortment of pets, alone in the day:
A goldfish, a lovebird, a dog and a cat,
Who was called Canterbury and here's more of that.

Its breed was a Manx, well known as the kind
That lack a tail from their collective behind.
"I should try and get one," he thought with a yawn
Just before lunch on a cold winter's morn.

So he walked over and declared with pride
To the dog, as his tummy began to rumble inside,
"I'm a Manx cat, Canterbury by name;
No tail do have I, which is such a shame.
Yet yours is so bendy and delightfully chic,
Do you think I could borrow it sometime this week?"

Barked the dog, "I'm sorry and I know it's not fair
But I need it to wag so I really can't share.
Please don't be sad – that would be absurd,
You could always go and ask the lovebird."

So Canterbury walked over and declared with pride
To the bird, as his tummy rumbled louder inside,
"I'm a Manx cat, Canterbury by name;
No tail do have I, which is such a shame.
Yet yours is so feathery and wonderfully green,
Perhaps you could lend it? Please don't be mean."

Chirped the bird, "I'm sorry and I know it's not fair
But I need it to fly so I really can't share.
I should like to help and make true your wish
And thus, I suggest you ask the goldfish."

So Canterbury walked over and declared with pride
To the fish, as his tummy rumbled more loudly inside,
"I'm a Manx cat, Canterbury by name;
No tail do have I, which is such a shame.
Yet yours is so dainty and brilliantly bright,
I'd love to have use of it just for one night."

Glugged the fish, "I'm sorry and I know it's not fair
But I need it to swim so I really can't share.
Now, do excuse me. Good luck with your task,
I'm sure there are others you still need to ask."

Canterbury stayed put though and hungrily eyed
The aquarium with the goldfish inside.
"Thanks for your help and don't think me rude
But I'm really quite famished and could do with some food.
I hope you won't mind if I'm perfectly frank:
You seem rather tasty as you swim round your tank."

Glugged the fish, "But I'd make such a trifling feast,
I think you should aim for a much larger beast.
I know you are hungry so why don't you try
Something delicious like feathered stir fry?"

So Canterbury walked back and hungrily eyed
The small cage with the lovebird inside.
"Hello again. Don't think me rude
But I'm really quite famished and could do with some food.
Let me be honest, I've got to the stage
Where you look very yummy as you sit in your cage."

Chirped the bird, "I'm much too small to consume!
Have something else that'll take up more room.
I'm sure you've been hungry for quite long enough:
Why not dine on a meal that comes with a woof?"

So Canterbury walked back and hungrily eyed
The dog with tail moving from side to side.
"Hello again. Don't think me rude
But I'm really quite famished and could do with some food.
When washed down with squash and plenty of ice,
I've heard that hot dogs are particularly nice."

Barked the dog, "Well, you know, I'm not sure about that."
And in one giant gulp, he swallowed the cat!
With lunch now complete, the dog could foresee
How much he'd enjoy fish and chirps for his tea.

Menu

Fishy

Birdy

Doggy

Switzerland is very nice –
That's what many people say.
I hope sometime to visit there
But maybe not today.
Nor perhaps tomorrow
And when, I do not know:
I'm stuck in school detention
And I'm not allowed to go.

A Visit to the Dentist

Toothache,
Dentist chair,
Where's the pain,
Here or there?
Lift your tongue,
Open wide…
Really need to
Get inside.
Put head back –
Do keep still!
Completely rotten,
Cannot fill.
Injection given,
Gums are froze,
In come pliers,
Out tooth goes.
Final rinse,
Free to go,
Any problems,
Let me know.
At reception,
Pay the fees.
Bye for now,
Next patient please!

The Highwayman

Dick Turpin used to cause distress,
He was a highwayman no less.
Once executed by the Law,
He was a highwayman no more!

TOPSY

This is a little story
About Topsy, my pet mouse,
Who was always free to roam
In the kitchen of my house.

One frightful day, fate intervened
When I was vacuuming around.
Somehow she got underneath
And was lifted off the ground.

I heard an awful *shlumpf* noise
As Topsy was sucked inside.
I opened up the cleaner,
Feeling sure she'd not survived.

However, in the workings,
Doomed Topsy was in luck:
She was very much alive
But seemed to be quite stuck.

I tugged and yanked with my hands,
How I heaved with all my might
And though I hoped to get her free,
The contraption held her tight.

Undeterred, I grabbed her tail
And with pliers I pulled some more
Till Topsy was released at last,
Looking *different* than before.

Her little face was still the same,
Yet here's the dreadful thing:
Her body was all stretched out
Like a furry piece of string!

She does come in handy though
When tying things together
And as a draught excluder,
She's good in windy weather.

I've also made a phone call,
Sent some photos that I took
And now she's the longest mouse
In the Guinness Records book.

tHE MESS

"Clean up all this mess at once!"
Shouted mother to the boy.
"And that includes all your books
And each and every toy.
I want this room spick and span,
Have I made that clear?
We must find grandma right away,
She's somewhere under here!"

Paint

People seem to dislike paint,
I don't know the reason why.
They say when something's boring,
It's like looking at it dry.
They say, "Watch out!" if it's wet
Or complain about the smell
But I think paint is lots of fun;
My family does as well.
It comes in many colours
Plus emulsion and gloss, too.
There's some that's mould-resistant
For your kitchen or your loo.
I can't see what there's to hate:
Paint's as good as any friend –
It's always there to lean on,
Sticking with you to the end.
So take your brush or roller,
Coat each ceiling, wall and door.
Should you happen to run out,
You can always buy some more.
I do hope that this message
To you is loud and clear.
From **John Smith of Smith & Co.**
(Paint Maker of the Year)

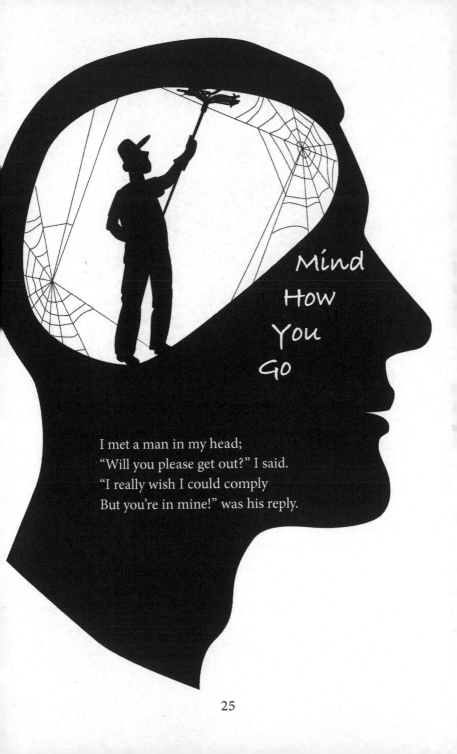

Mind How You Go

I met a man in my head;
"Will you please get out?" I said.
"I really wish I could comply
But you're in mine!" was his reply.

The Fairy

At the bottom of my garden,
Surprised was I to see
A lovely little fairy girl,
Whose name was Emily.

"Hello," said I, when first I spied
Her sitting on a rose.
She looked up with her tiny eyes
And twitched her tiny nose.

Her nostrils proved quite magical
For I was shrunk in height
And I became as small as she:
It gave me such a fright.

The fairy introduced herself
And then began to cry.
I gently put her hand in mine
And asked the reason why.

"It should be plain to you," she sobbed.
"My name – it does offend:
The others make such fun of me
That I have not a friend.

Fairies should have pretty names
Like Skugboolay and Gloo
And Drippleblot and Fluttypapp
And Rasketponky, too."

"Those names are quite absurd," I said.
"Yours is far the best
And I will be your pal for life
So please don't be depressed."

Much time has passed since first we met;
I see her still each day.
But now, we're not on speaking terms:
My best friend is Skugboolay!

On a budget to catch some crooks?
The cheapest in the Hero books
Is Super Squad, who wage war with wrong
(Providing that it won't take long).
The team includes the 'Justice Clown',
Whose custard pies take evil down.
'The Blizz', meanwhile, can enshroud
Baddies in her dandruff cloud.
The man in charge is 'Captain Breath':
His mouthy smells cause instant death.
They're ready, standing by to act,
With costumes pressed and cases packed,
But should the thieves somehow get free,
Whatever you do, don't blame me!

MISS WINTER'S DEMISE

"A crime's been committed,
The victim is dead
And one of you killed her!"
Inspector Drew said.
"I have gathered you here
In this room today
To inform the murderer,
They won't get away.
Let's look at the facts
Of Miss Winter's demise.
We know that someone

Poisoned her favourite pies.
Indeed, a mere mouthful
Was enough to combust
The unlucky victim
To a small pile of dust.
But just who would gain
From her sudden expiry?
That clearly must
Be my line of enquiry.
I have looked at her will
And know to be true,
She left sums of money
To each one of you."
At this, the four suspects
Shared a grave look:
The butler, the maid,
The gardener, the cook.
They shifted uncomfortably
And squirmed in their seats
As Inspector Drew tried
To detect their deceits.
Greenslade, the butler,
Was first to declare,
"I am quite innocent
For I was elsewhere."
"That's right!" said another,
"He had the day off
With a rather bad cold
And a terrible cough."
The maid, Caroline,
Was next to speak,

"It wasn't me either,
I've been gone the whole week.
I skived off to Paris,"
She told the keen sleuth,
"And here is my passport
To prove it's the truth."
Meanwhile, the gardener,
Known as Blind Jim,
Was so frail and arthritic
That Drew dismissed him.
To the armchair detective,
Jim's lack of sight
Suggested the cop
Was probably right.
By ruling them out,
There was one suspect still:
"Brenda the cook!"
He proclaimed with a shrill.
Said Brenda, abashed,
"I admit that it's true
I cannot remember
The things that I do.
If the others are blameless,
Then it can only be me
And perhaps, by mistake,
I served gunpowder at tea."
The Inspector looked pleased
For now she'd confessed,
He had some good grounds
To make an arrest.
With 'cuffs on her wrists,

She was led to the clink
And was highly embarrassed
By what people must think.
With the case thus closed,
The staff went to bed:
All out of a job
Since their employer was dead.
With the killer in jail,
Caught by The Bill,
Miss Winter's large house
Stood empty and still,
Save for the opening
Of a secret trapdoor
That lay hidden beneath
The drawing room floor.
And as she emerged,
Miss Winter laughed.
She'd ridded herself
Of her workers at last:
The forgetful cook,
The absentee maid,
The decrepit gardener
And the sickly Greenslade.
But this tale has a moral
For whilst mowing the lawn,
Miss Winter was caught
In a big thunderstorm.
As she hurried inside,
A great lightning flash
Struck both house and Miss Winter
And reduced them to ash.

The Bear at the Door

Ding-dong, ding-dong, ding-dong!
A bear has rung our bell.
I watched as it came along;
My sister did as well.

Rat-a-tat-tat-tat-tat!
It's knocking now, I fear.
Should I go and answer that
Or claim I didn't hear?

"Hello! Hello! Hello!"
Bears can't speak, however.
Thus, it only goes to show
This one must be quite clever.

Phut-phut, phut-phut, phut-phut!
That sounds like the letter flap.
Should I take a closer look?
Or maybe it's a trap.

But wait, there is a note
From mum addressed to me:
She says she's in her fur coat,
Locked out (allegedly).

Perhaps I should take care:
The writing might be fake
And letting in a clever bear
Would be a huge mistake!

Professor MacCavity

Professor MacCavity
Objected to gravity
But his theories failed to convince.
So to prove he was right,
He jumped from a great height
And no-one has heard from him since.

A CONCERNED CHILD

I've got to ring the doctor,
My dad's not well you see.
In his throat, he's got a frog
And we have to set it free.

Dad also has some butterflies,
Which he says are in his tum.
I've tried to tempt them out with leaves
But they've refused to come.

Perhaps I'll tell the doctor
About his crow's feet, too.
I'm sure we could stick them back
On the bird with superglue.

When the doctor's finished though
And dad's allowed back home,
I know mum has a blocked up nose
So there's a plumber I must phone.

THE APPLE

I'm a juicy apple
That dangles from a tree,
With skin a lovely green
I'm bound to be tasty.
Pick me from the tall branch
And take a few big bites.
I really wouldn't mind, you know...
I'm not much good with heights!

 # THE FLY

How rude! How rude!
There's a fly on my food –
A real infection machine.
I must get a swatter
And squash that rotter.
God only knows where he's been!

But this fly is most clever
As he avoids my endeavour
To swipe him away from my plate.
He buzzes around
Like an airborne greyhound,
Doing his best to frustrate.

After almost an hour,
I use some brainpower
And grab the insecticide can.
I give a slight snigger
As I press on the trigger
And start to action my plan.

But my hands are misplaced
And it sprays in my face,
My aim being clearly off track.
So the fly wins the war
And escapes through a door,
Though I'll get him when next he comes back.

MR RAT

Hello Mr Rat, my friend,
You're looking very smart
And may I say how well you dress –
That bow tie looks just the part.
Off somewhere nice perhaps?
A tour of local inns?
Oh I see, you're dining out,
Going through some bins.
I'm eating out myself, you know,
Rated highly by reviewers:
A quite delightful place, I've heard,
With views of open sewers.
I suppose I should get going now,
We should meet soon, however.
How about the Underground?
We could catch the drain together.

THE ROOM OF DOOM

Mr and Mrs McFerguson-Slack
Rented a place in a nice cul-de-sac.
The owner (an inventor) had just gone away
To somewhere mysterious but no-one would say.

The couple moved in and were exploring the house
When the husband, in puzzlement, called to his spouse
That he'd found a strange room upon the first floor,
Where a sign saying 'PRIVATE' hung from the door.

Inside, by a wardrobe, just to the right,
Was a red button, glowing brightly with light.
Being quite baffled, they gave it a press –
A choice that resulted in major distress.

At first nothing happened, save for a sound:
A humming of sorts that echoed around.
The Room seemed to blur with a mechanical moan
As sparks danced about like a circuit had blown.

Suddenly the pair were shocked to be squeezed
Into the Queen's bath: she looked most displeased.
They mouthed a quick sorry to the royal concerned
When everything shimmered and The Room was returned.

"Did that really happen?" the wife loudly screamed.
"Or was it just something we both merely dreamed?"
Before her dazed husband had chance to report,
The sparking resumed and they commenced teleport.

"Leave us alone!" bellowed the couple in rage
As they both reappeared in some form of cage.
But then they fell silent for they saw with their eyes
They shared it with lions of formidable size.

This, they assumed, was the end of the line
And they would be eaten by a giant feline.
So they were amazed and relieved, to be sure,
To find themselves back in The Room as before.

The McFerguson-Slacks, in the space of an hour,
Visited the Alps plus the famed Eiffel Tower,
The Great Wall of China during a scary typhoon,
And thankfully a toilet (which was over too soon).

Then off again, somewhere else on the globe.
"Oh curse that red button beside the wardrobe
And curse the inventor who created The Room!"
Shouted the husband, continuing to fume.

The unfortunate pair are still bouncing around:
At the moment, I believe they're Siberia-bound.
As for The Room, a rogue silicon chip
Had allowed only one proper hyperspeed trip.

And that single jump was made by the chap,
Who had built The Room before the mishap.
Leaving instructions for his house to be let,
He'd beamed to Hawaii and isn't back yet.

ALFIE

I have a dog called Alfie –
Of his breed, I have no clue.
In fact, I'm rather puzzled
Why his coat's that shade of blue.
Both his tails are spiky sharp
And his ears light up at night.
He's got over twenty legs –
That surely can't be right!
I'm pleased he has just one pair
Of delightful, happy eyes
But they fire off laser beams
Whenever he's surprised.
His bark is like the loudest belch
And he never fetches ball –
Maybe, when I think of it,
He's not a dog at all.

The Pirates

The *Wet Fish* was a pirate ship,
With sails that billowed in the breeze
And aboard was the nicest crew
You could meet upon the seas.

They never looted any boats
And gold, they'd never take,
For they would rather sit around
With tea and angel cake.

Blackhead was the captain,
Admired by all his men
Even though he made them be
In bed by half past ten.*

Other buccaneers, however,
Thought Blackhead brought them shame:
His crew was far too pleasant
And gave pirates a bad name.

Eventually it was decided at
The Skull and Crossbones Ball
That Blackhead and his shipmates
Were not welcome there at all.

They were also told to leave
The trade without delay
And find very different jobs
Someplace far away.

And so it was that Blackhead
Turned his back upon the ocean.
He became a first rate salesman
Selling suntan lotion.

In fact, he made a lot of cash,
Which he knew he should invest
But being a pirate still at heart,
It went in his treasure chest!

*or eleven o'clock on Saturdays

45

 # HARRY PUGH

"I'm really bored," whined Harry Pugh,
"There's nothing here for me to do.
I used to get so many thrills
By pulling heads off daffodils
Or hanging outside corner shops
With my gang in hoodie tops,
Shouting out at passers-by
While pretending to be samurai.
It used to be a massive lark
To kick the litter round the park.
Lately though, it's not as fun
Being such a hooligan.
Perhaps I'm just too old these days –
At least that's what my grandson says.
Maybe I should start afresh
And get myself a new address,
Where no-one's ever heard of me
Or of my delinquency:
No more arrests or county courts,
No more long parole reports,
Just sipping tea in an old folks' home,
Watching films in monochrome.
That would suit me fine, I'm sure
And prove I'm not so immature.
Getting there would be the worst…
I'd have to steal some transport first."

Waiting

"How long's a piece of string?" mum said,
When I asked how long she'd be.
I didn't know the answer
So I went downstairs to see.
I hunted through each kitchen drawer
And then found some on a shelf.
It was almost five foot seven:
I measured it myself.
I ran back up the stairs to mum
So I could tell her what I knew
But she said I'd still have to wait
Another inch or maybe two.

Gone Fishing

I pleaded with my father
To take me fishing in the bay.
I really wish I hadn't
As we had an awful day.

We only caught three tyres,
Some underpants and tins,
Lots of bottles filled with rum
And several wheelie bins.

If only we had given up
After reeling in that spade…
But no! We carried on and hooked
An extremely cross mermaid.

We offered sincere apologies,
Which we hoped would be accepted.
Instead, she just droned on and on
How her species was protected.

She even had a copy
Of the law for us to view
And directed our attention
Towards Section 32.

"Anglers must refrain," she read,
"By the Government's own decree,
Of catching any mermaids
Within the open sea.

Those who fail to adhere
To the rules in this regard
Should be reported straight away
To the police or coastal guard."

In the end, we paid her off
And she promised to keep mum
In exchange for the underpants,
All the tyres and the rum.

As she dived back in the water,
We were glad of no more fuss,
Though dad and I have both agreed
That fishing's not for us.

THE RESTLESS NIGHT

Last night when in bed,
I rested my head
Upon my favourite pillow.
But it didn't feel soft
So I held it aloft
And found a small armadillo.

He was curled in a heap
So I left him to sleep
And went to the room kept for guests.
But when climbing the bunk,
I stepped on the trunk
Of an elephant in her nightdress.

I escaped through the gloom
To my brother's bedroom
As he was out till next day.
But imagine my shock
When I saw a large croc
Napping beneath the duvet.

There was nothing for me
Except the settee
And I crept downstairs full of hope.
But I had been beat
For there on the seat
Were some slumbering antelope.

Ending up on the floor,
I tried hard to ignore
All the animal drool and spittle.
I try not to complain
But it's often a pain
That my dad is Dr Dolittle.

Nonets

(9 lines of poetry containing 9 syllables, 8 syllables, 7 syllables, 6 syllables, 5 syllables, 4 syllables, 3 syllables, 2 syllables and 1 syllable)

#1 ✗

I think nonets are quite hard to write
And though I work on them each night,
Checking that they really rhyme
Takes up lots of my time;
But what truly drives
Me round the bend
Is that word
Right at
The

#2 ✓

I think nonets are quite hard to write
And though I work on them each night,
Checking that they really rhyme
Takes up lots of my time;
But what truly drives
Me round the bend
Is that word
At the
End.

52

Simply Magic

I've magic fingers
And magic toes,
Magic shoulders,
A magic nose,
Magic legs
To magic run
Because I am
A magician.

A Great British Tradition

There's a super medicine
That seems to cure most ills.
It isn't an injection though
Or a box of little pills.

It's a delicious steaming cup
Of liquid, hot and brown,
Designed to lift your spirits
Even when you're feeling down.

Miracles are hard to find
But if you look, you'll see
The answer's right in front of you:
It's a good old fashioned tea.

You can drink it almost any time,
Morning, noon or night.
Got something to celebrate?
Then tea will see you right!

You can add both milk and sugar,
You can have it with some ice,
You can add a dash of lemon,
Which I find to be quite nice.

Forget all other beverages,
The tea leaf rules the scene.
Coffee is but second rate,
An 'also ran' has-bean.

You just can't beat a cup of tea,
It's what everybody thinks.
It truly is the hot drink of kings
And the king of all hot drinks.

(Except my daughter says hot chocolate is better)

A GRiM TALE

Now gather round my children,
There's a grim tale to be told.
It might make your eyes pop out
Or turn your blood ice-cold.
I had it from my grandpapa
And from my father, too;
My uncle had it also,
Now I'm passing it to you.
You wonder what I talk of?
Well, it's time you learnt the truth:

All of us have stinky feet,
Which seem to be soap-proof!
You must have surely wondered
About those clouds of green
That waft right up from your toes
Even though you're sure they're clean.
Have problems when in shoe shops?
Do flowers wilt when you're nearby?
I can tell you here and now,
Your feet are the reason why!
Doesn't matter if they're enclosed
By a sock or welly boot,
The safest way to get up close
Is in a biohazard suit.
But should you wish to make new friends,
The advice with which I'd begin,
Is to do what your mother does
And tell them, "Don't breathe in!"

MUD

What is this mud in which I stand,
Which seems to cover all the land
From riverbank to mountain crest,
From north to south and east to west?
A realm of brown, a gloopy brew,
Like chocolate paint or gravy glue.
It's fed by rain and starved by drought
And now I'm in it, I can't get out!
A careless step from solid ground,
Heralded by a slurping sound,
Saw both my feet pulled from below,
With my knees the next to go.
And though I fought its gooey grip,
It pulled me right down to my hip.
Ever rising, it sucks me in:
My chest, my neck and now my chin.
My doom is but a muddy hug,
Goodbye cruel world!
      Glug!
           Glug!
                Glug!

BONSAI

Bonsai
trees are little
plants, smaller than dogs,
bigger than ants. I chopped
one down the other day
but "Timb-" was
all
I'd
time
to
say

THE NAGGYBOO

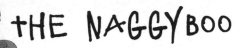

I hate the naughty Naggyboo
That live beneath my bed
For when my room is nice and neat,
They mess it up instead.

They sprinkle dust onto my shelves,
Hide sweets in every drawer;
They throw my clothes into a heap
And spread crumbs across the floor.

They doodle on my homework,
Squirt ink over my hands
But when I tell the teacher,
She just never understands.

I'm fairly sure my parents know
About the Naggyboo
Because looking at their bedroom,
I think they have them, too.

My Name is Ziller Vorgon

My name is Ziller Vorgon,
I'm an alien, cruel and mean:
A cybernetic creature
That's half squid and half machine.

But look beyond my armoured shell
And you will find, no doubt,
Something tender-hearted,
Which is trying to get out.

For what I seek is romance:
A mechanical alliance
With a warm, non-smoking
Electrical appliance.

If you're a single oven,
Who is evil, through and through,
Why not get in touch with me?
I'd love to hear from you.

We'll rule galaxies together,
Destroy worlds until we're spent
With my destructive death ray
And your heating element.

I'd be your darling husband
For all eternity
But if you'd rather we stay at home,
Then that would still suit me.

Gramps

My grandad hasn't got much hair,
In truth, his head is almost bare.
He keeps it free from dirt and grime
By using polish all the time.
Then, no matter what the weather,
He'll buff it up with chamois leather.
But since he rubs it every day,
Grandad has worn his head away:
Despite him being six foot tall,
His head is like a ping pong ball!
He doesn't really seem to mind
And likes the fact it's super-shined.
But when sunrays bounce off my gramps,
He's lit up like a thousand lamps,
Blinding cars and passers-by
And any airplanes in the sky.
Even spacemen, so it is said,
Have seen the glare from grandad's head.
And when the sun goes down at night,
Moonbeams still keep his scalp alight.
So he's moving to the coast
To take up an important post:
Warning ships of rocks and sand –
The finest lighthouse in the land.

Sherlock

Said Sherlock Holmes to Watson,
"The solution's plain to see –
There are just so many clues
That it's elementary."
Though Watson did not answer,
He gave Holmes a prompting cough,
As if to say, "Please go on
Before I go dozing off."
"The culprit, my dear fellow,"
The detective then replied,
"Has some specific features
Which cannot be denied.
Being rather short in height,
The felon of this crime
Is really rather quiet,
At least for the present time.
He thought himself so clever,
As cunning as a fox,
But now I know the criminal
Who stole toffees from my box.
I'd placed it on the high shelf
So he'd have stood on tippytoes
But he only took the front sweets
And none from the other rows.
Had this rogue been taller then

He'd have snatched a bigger share
So I deduce he must be small
As he left the back ones there.
Furthermore, I see the lid
Has been hastily replaced
So assuming he was disturbed,
Then this bounder can be traced;
For it seems quite reasonable
That the villain of this piece
Might have a chewy toffee
Still stuck between his teeth.
If that is that so, dear Watson,"
Remarked the famous sleuth,
"He has to keep his mouth shut
Or risk showing me the truth.
If I need to spell it out,
I'm of the firmest view
That the evidence all seems to point
To the robber being you.
"Ot ahuns ow?" mumbled Watson
As toffee still clamped his jaw.
"What happens now," said Holmes,
"Is we're going to eat some more."

OLD TOM

When old Tom was ninety-three,
He caught some form of leprosy,
Which started with a hacking cough
Until he hacked his head clean off.
The medics came and fought in vain
To join his body parts again.
Glue and tape were even tried
And in the end, he would have died
Were it not for cotton thread,
Which sewed Tom's neck back to his head.
Though just as quick as he was patched,
Each of his limbs became detached.
Sadly, the doctors were dumbfound,
By all the bits that lay around:
They stitched on arms where legs should be
(Knowing little of anatomy)
And whilst I'm pleased to declare
That Tom is not beyond repair,
He must stay in, day and night,
Until the surgeons put him right.
Only once a year he's seen…
They let him out on Halloween!

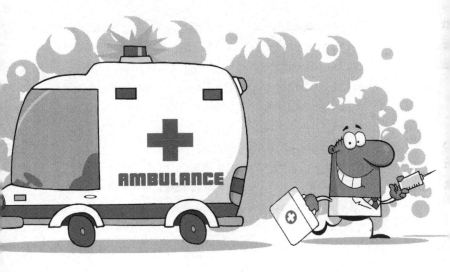

About the Author

Paul Minton has always wanted to be a writer. He has also wanted to be a policeman, a doctor, a lawyer and a steam locomotive running somewhere near the seaside. He has had funny stories published in Canada, nonfiction articles printed in Great Britain and poetry broadcast in Australia. He has been a runner up four times at the All Wales Comic Verse Competition and appeared on Channel Four's quiz show *Fifteen to One* when he was asked a very difficult question about religious dictionaries (which he got wrong!) He is married with a daughter and lives in South Wales with a West Highland terrier, a tortoise and a large number of woodlice that he seems unable to get rid of.

You can contact Paul either by email at cherrytreechips@gmail.com or by tweeting him via @cherrytreechips. He'd really rather prefer it if you didn't just turn up at his front door.

Index of First Lines